ANCIENT

GREECE

PETER HICKS

RSVP

RAINTREE
STECK-VAUGHN
PUBLISHERS
A Steck-Vaughn Company

Austin, Texas

History Beneath Your Feet

Titles in this series

Ancient Egypt
Ancient Greece
Ancient Rome
The Aztecs

Published by Raintree Steck-Vaughn Publishers, an imprint of Steck-Vaughn Company

Library of Congress Cataloging-in-Publication Data
Hicks, Peter.
Ancient Greece / Peter Hicks.
    p.   cm.—(History beneath your feet)
    Includes bibliographical references and index.
    Summary: Highlights the many archaeological digs and findings in Greece and discusses what life was like in ancient Greece.
    ISBN 0-8172-5750-0
    1. Greece—Antiquities—Juvenile literature.
    2. Excavations (Archaeology)—Greece— Juvenile literature.
    3. Greece—Civilization—To 146 B.C.— Juvenile literature.
    [1. Greece—Antiquities. 2. Greece—Civilization— To 146 B.C.]
    I. Title. II. Series.
    DF78.H58 1999
    938—dc21   99-17132

Printed in Italy. Bound in the United States.
1 2 3 4 5 6 7 8 9 0 03 02 01 00 99

Cover photographs: The Tholos at Delphi (Michael Holford); "Mask of Agamemnon" (AKG)

llustrations and project artwork: John Yates

The publishers would like to thank the following for permission to publish their pictures

Lesley & Roy Adkins 19, 21, 24, 32; AKG (London) 6, 7, 9, 10, 18, 30, 36, 37; Ancient Art and Architecture Collection 28; C.M. Dixon 14, 23, 26; Robert Harding 4–5, 16, 38; Peter Hicks 11, 17, 41, 42; Michael Holford 15, 22, 33; Norma Joseph 8, 12–13, 40, 43; Planet Earth Pictures 34; John Prague, The Manchester Museum, University of Manchester 31, 35; Wayland Picture Library 27, 39

CONTENTS

WHAT IS ARCHAEOLOGY?

"Archaeology" is a Greek word meaning "the study of ancient things." Archaeologists study the remains of people, buildings, and objects from earlier times and then piece together what life had been like in the past. Some of these remains are so old that they have become hidden by earth or more recent buildings. This means that archaeologists first have to find where these remains are hidden, and then dig down or excavate to see what is there. This is why so much history is "beneath your feet."

WHO WERE THE ANCIENT GREEKS?

Greece is a beautiful, mountainous country surrounded by the sea. Only about 20 percent of the land is suitable for growing crops, making agriculture very difficult. Even the Mediterranean Sea—essential for food and transportation—contains strong currents and winds that test the best sailors.

MACEDONIA

Pella

Vergina • Olynthus

Troy

AEGEAN SEA

ASIA MINOR

Delphi •

Corinth • • Athens

Olympia • • Mycenae

Pylos •

IONIAN SEA

PELOPONNESE

Knossos

CRETE

The ancient Greeks lived on the mainland and islands of Greece and also colonized other parts of the ancient world. The harshness of their country may be why they achieved so much. Through hard work their settlements became prosperous—often in the face of terrible disasters such as earthquakes, famine, plague, and war.

The civilization now called Classical Greece began around 650 B.C. At this time Greece was not one country but was made up of many independent "city states," each of which was called a *polis*. Despite the fact that the city states were often at war with one another, together they produced exceptional art, architecture, theater, poetry, music, and philosophy, as well as the now world-famous Olympic Games.

What we know about the ancient Greeks has had to be pieced together from the evidence that remains: ruins of their buildings, ancient inscriptions and writings, and individual artifacts. This is the job of the archaeologist.

The ruins of the temple of Apollo at Corinth

EARLY CIVILIZATIONS IN GREECE

The first civilization of the Greek world was on the island of Crete. The inhabitants became very wealthy by trading their wheat, olive oil, and wine with other parts of the Mediterranean. Around 2000 B.C., large, impressive palaces were built at Knossos, Phaistos, and Zakros.

The restored throne room at Knossos with its beautiful wall paintings. Sir Arthur Evans thought the throne belonged to a woman so he called it the "Throne of Ariadne" (the daughter of King Minos).

HOW PALACES AND CITIES ARE "LOST"

When a palace or city is abandoned—or destroyed, as Knossos was—a number of things may happen.

- It may be "robbed" of building materials for use in other buildings.

- Even if this does not happen, over time roof timbers rot, roofs collapse onto the floor, and the weakened walls fall in on themselves.

- The site may be leveled and new buildings are placed over the original foundations.

- In the countryside, soil and vegetation will build up or grow over the remains, hiding them completely.

The civilization on Crete lasted for over a thousand years until it was destroyed by two key events. Around 1626 B.C. the volcanic island of Thera, 56 mi. (90 km) north of Crete, erupted, causing flooding and earthquakes that destroyed many buildings. Then, around 1450 B.C., fierce warriors from Mycenae on mainland Greece conquered Crete.

An English archaeologist, Sir Arthur Evans (1851–1941), began excavating the Palace of Knossos in 1900. The palace ruins covered 5.4 acres, and the ground plan suggested the labyrinth associated with the legendary King Minos. As a result, Evans called the civilization of Crete "Minoan."

Evans is regarded as one of the first "scientific" archaeologists to work in Greece. He kept a detailed log book or "site diary" of his work, and pioneered the use of photography to record the stages of the dig. He built high observation towers so that the whole site could easily be photographed. Up to that time archaeologists had only made sketches of sites, and then only when they came across a major find. The great advantage of photographs is that they provide a quick and accurate record of a site long after finds have been removed to museums or the diggings have been filled in again.

Sir Arthur Evans, the excavator of Knossos. He is holding a copy of a bull's head found at the bottom of a well.

THE MYCENAEANS

The Mycenaeans who invaded Crete came from the southern part of the Greek mainland, known as the Peloponnese. Graves found on the mainland tell us that theirs was a wealthy civilization based on trade over land and sea. The remains of weapons show that they built up a large army, equipped with bronze plate armor. The poet Homer tells us that it was the king of Mycenae who led the Greeks against the city of Troy in Asia Minor (Turkey)—the legendary Trojan War.

The exact site of the city of Troy remained unidentified until modern times. This was partly because archaeologists thought that the Trojan legend was no more than that, and that "Troy" did not exist at all.

The German archaeologist Heinrich Schliemann proved them wrong. Between 1870 and 1890 he excavated on a large scale at the "Hisarlik mound" in Turkey, which he believed was the site of the legendary city. Because he thought that Troy must be in the lowest level of the mound, he carelessly dug through the upper levels, destroying a great deal of valuable evidence.

Schliemann was desperate to find the grave of Agamemnon, the Mycenaean commander of the Greek force. At Mycenae in 1876, ignoring all the wishes of the Greek government who wanted a small dig, he smashed his way through the site, destroying important Greek and Roman remains. Discovering five shaft graves inside the acropolis, he found enough treasure "to fill a museum."

The shaft graves at Mycenae. The ancient Greek poet Homer's comment that "Mycenae was rich in gold" was proved correct by Schliemann, who found numerous gold artifacts in the graves.

PROJECT: THE GOLD "MASK OF AGAMEMNON"

You will need:
Modeling clay
Gold or yellow paint
Varnish
Toothpick

1. Make a ball about the size of your fist from the modeling clay.

2. Flatten and shape the ball so that it will cover your face.

3. Make and shape two sausages of clay for the lips. Make and shape another sausage for the nose. Attach these to the mask.

4. Shape two balls of clay for the ears and two more for the eyes. Attach to the mask.

5. Use the toothpick to scratch on the eyebrows, beard, and mustache.

6. Paint the mask gold (or yellow). Allow to dry, then varnish.

Schliemann was convinced a gold-masked body was Agamemnon. Unfortunately, the mask was 300 years older than the Trojan War (which probably took place around 1250 B.C.) and there were rumors that Schliemann had "planted" some of the finds.

The lavish gold mask found in one of the graves of Mycenae. Schliemann claimed it was the "face of Agamemnon" but some archaeologists believe he added the mustache to make it more king-like.

CLASSICAL GREECE

In time, the Mycenaeans grew weaker and tribes invaded Greece from the north. By 1100 B.C. most Mycenaean towns and palaces had been destroyed or abandoned. Greece entered a period known as the "dark age," because no written evidence has survived to tell archaeologists and historians about what happened during that time.

The dark age lasted until about 800 B.C. By 650 B.C. Greece had begun to prosper again, and the city states were founded. Temples and public buildings were constructed and cities flourished. The Greeks established colonies in southern Italy, Sicily, western Turkey, and parts of north Africa. The age of "Classical Greece" had begun.

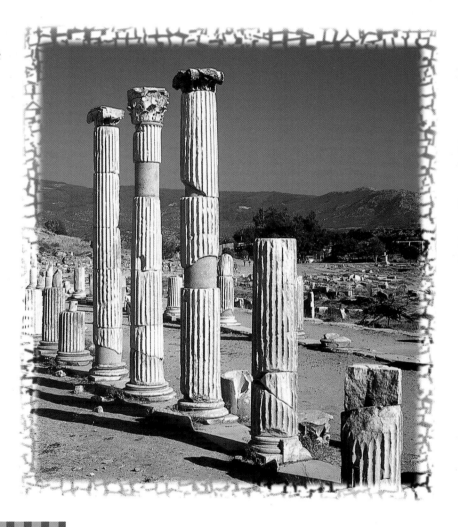

The agora, or marketplace, at Ephesus. Although in Anatolia (modern-day Turkey), Ephesus was regarded as an important city in the Greek homeland.

JOHN TURTLE WOOD

In 1860 the British Museum funded the railroad engineer John Turtle Wood to search for treasures in Greece. He discovered and excavated the Temple of Artemis at Ephesus. He calculated that he shifted 132,227 cubic feet of "spoil." How much important evidence—pottery, metal objects, human remains—was thrown away in the process it is impossible to guess.

The remains of classical Greece have always fascinated Europeans, but during the late nineteenth and early twentieth centuries this fascination turned into a craze. Treasure hunters plundered Greece of its valuable artifacts, sending them to museums in their home countries. There was much rivalry among museums to obtain the "best" finds. Because the museums funded many of the expeditions, they were able to put pressure on the "archaeologists" to unearth treasures as quickly as possible. This did not encourage careful excavation.

FIELD WALKING

Unlike the treasure hunters of the nineteenth century, modern archaeologists are extremely scientific and methodical in their search for the history beneath our feet. A suspected site is often "field walked" before any digging begins. This involves close inspection of the ground. An area is divided into grid squares, and each walker has to scour the surface of assigned squares for pottery, brick, tile, or glass—in fact, any manmade objects. These may be evidence of a site underground, and where these surface finds run out might mark the boundary of the site.

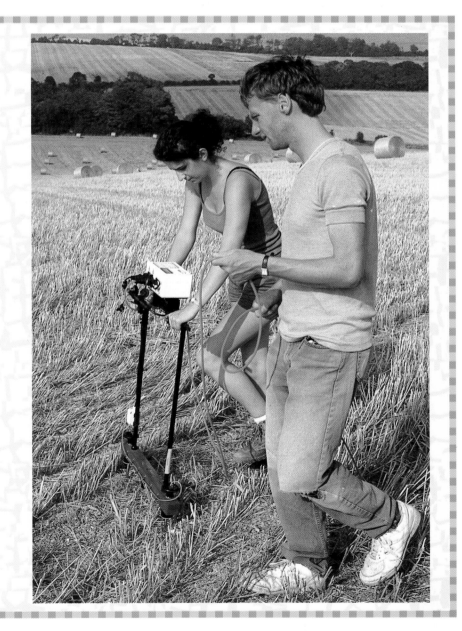

After field walking, archaeologists search for structures under the surface. This resistivity meter passes an electric current into the ground. High resistance may suggest a building, low resistance a ditch or pit.

THE THEATER AT EPIDAURUS

Archaeologists are tremendously interested in Classical Greece because it is regarded as the beginning of European civilization. The work and ideas of its mathematicians, philosophers, playwrights, architects, writers, and artists have had a huge impact on the Western world.

For example, our modern theater owes a lot to Classical Greece. The word itself comes from the Greek *theatron*, meaning "seeing place." Careful excavation of ancient Greek theaters has led to a greater understanding of how they worked. The best preserved and most famous ancient Greek theater is at Epidaurus in the Peloponnese. It is still used today for performances of Greek tragedies and comedies.

Archaeologists found that the theater at Epidaurus consisted of a huge "orchestra"—75 ft. (23 m) in diameter—in which the chorus danced and sang. The actors stood on a raised stage called a *proskension*, 80 ft. (24 m) long by 8 ft. (2.5 m) wide. Behind this, archaeologists discovered the *skene*—the actors' changing room, from which we got our word "scene."

The excavations showed that the auditorium (seating area) was built in two phases. The first phase consisted of 34 rows of seats, which held 6,200 spectators. Later another 24 rows were added, increasing the capacity to 12,300. The whole theater, carved into the side of Mount Konyortos, is a breathtaking sight.

The theater at Epidaurus covers a huge area and the seats are divided into 12 sections. The theater was badly damaged by the invading Goths in A.D. 267.

RESTORATION TECHNIQUES

Ancient buildings are often badly damaged and need to be restored. When the theater at Epidaurus was excavated, it was found that the support walls and seating at the edges had collapsed. Working up from the original foundations and using similar stone, archaeologists were able to rebuild the damaged areas.

ATHENS

By the middle of the fifth century B.C., Athens had become the largest and wealthiest city state in the Classical Greek world and had an impressive army and navy. The city expanded from the famous Acropolis, a high, rocky outcrop that was a natural fortress strengthened by huge stone walls. As the city grew, the central marketplace, known as the agora, became an increasingly important civic and religious center. It was surrounded by government buildings such as council chambers and law courts and contained two "stoas": covered market halls to shelter traders and shoppers in hot or wet weather.

THE AGORA

By the early twentieth century the agora had completely disappeared under the houses of 7,000 modern Athenians. More and more people were coming to live in Athens, and in 1924 the Greek government decided to excavate the agora before it was too late. However they did not have enough money to buy out all the inhabitants, tear down their houses, and begin digging! Fortunately, in 1927 the American millionaire John D. Rockefeller donated $250,000 to the government, allowing the project to go ahead.

The agora and stoa of Attalos in Athens, dominated by the Acropolis. The stoa was rebuilt by American archaeologists in the 1930s and today is a museum housing the finds from the agora.

The excavation was carried out by the American School of Classical Studies. They demolished 365 buildings and between 1931 and 1939 dug 250,000 tons of "spoil." It was a well-organized excavation, which showed that much of the agora consisted of stores, workshops, and stalls that sold items such as pots, bronze and marble statues, lamps, shoes, olive oil, meat, and fish.

Evidence of Athenian democracy was also found at the agora. An "allotment machine" was discovered, which was used to choose jury members randomly for trials. Water clocks were also found, which were used to time the speeches made in court. Speeches were timed so that those for the defense and those for the prosecution were always the same length, making sure that trials were fair and balanced.

Excavations being carried out at the agora in Athens

STRATIGRAPHY

An archaeological site like the agora in Athens usually has different "layers of occupation." The deeper the layer, the older it is, and any artifact discovered in a lower layer will be older than those nearer the surface. When archaeologists cut a "section" through a site (which looks a bit like a layer cake with a slice removed), all the strata (layers) can be seen and understood. Pottery, coins, and other artifacts found at each level help archaeologists decide how old that level is.

An archaeological "section." Can you figure out the oldest and most recent objects?

THE ACROPOLIS

The buildings of the Acropolis have always been of great interest to archaeologists because of what they tell us about ancient Greek life.

The most famous building is the Parthenon, which was completed in 432 B.C. and is a temple dedicated to Athena, the goddess of wisdom, arts, and crafts.

When it was excavated, archaeologists found that the interior of the Parthenon contained a very large inner shrine (called a *cella*), divided into two rooms. Ancient Greek writings told archaeologists that the east room once contained a 40-ft. (12-m) high statue of Athena made of solid gold. They found evidence of this in the form of a rectangular depression in the ground where the statue probably once stood.

The Acropolis (which means "high city"), seen from the southwest. It stands on a huge limestone cliff over 500 ft. (153 m) tall, 870 ft. (265 m) long, and 500 ft. (153 m) wide.

The smaller west room originally housed the women who served Athena, although Greek writers tell us that this was later used as the treasury of Athens.

Excavations have uncovered a large number of animal bones: the remains of sacrifices to the goddess. Other items used for worship have also been discovered, such as marble and bronze statues, bowls, marble basins, and altars.

Figures from the left side of the east pediment of the Parthenon. The male figure is thought to be Heracles or Dionysus while the women are the goddesses Demeter, Persephone, and Hebe.

THE ELGIN MARBLES

Lord Thomas Elgin (1766–1841), a British diplomat and art collector, was sent to Athens to collect works of art and to prevent France from dominating this "trade." In July 1801 Elgin ordered the seizing of the last remaining statues from the Parthenon and other parts of the Acropolis, as well as 55 marble slabs from a frieze in the Parthenon. Many people, notably the famous poet Lord Byron, were outraged at what they saw as vandalism, but Elgin argued that he had permission from the Turkish government. Because the Turks were occupying Greece at that time, the Greek authorities were powerless to stop the theft of their archaeological heritage. In 1816 Elgin sold the marbles to the British Museum, in London, where they can still be seen.

CITIES AND TOWNS

The Greeks were great city builders, but although many cities were built in Greece and its colonies, none have survived intact. Many were destroyed by enemies of the Greeks, especially the Romans, and the remains of most of them are hidden beneath other settlements built during the last 2,500 years. However, archaeologists have managed to excavate within modern cities and discover classical remains, and they have found abandoned settlements in the countryside where foundations were hidden by soil and vegetation.

The impressive city of Argos in southern Greece flourished between the seventh and third centuries B.C. Careful excavation has revealed the city's agora, with its council chamber, hall, shrine, *odeon* (a small theater for music and poetry recitals), and theater.

The south entrance of the agora at Corinth. There were 33 stores there, and, from the evidence of the jugs and cups found, most of them sold wine!

Archaeology has taught us that many Greek colonies throughout the Mediterranean were heavily based on farming. Aerial photographs of the town of Metapontum in southern Italy have revealed numerous field boundaries and farms, which surrounded the coastal town. The grain produced by farming communities like this was shipped home to feed the growing Greek population.

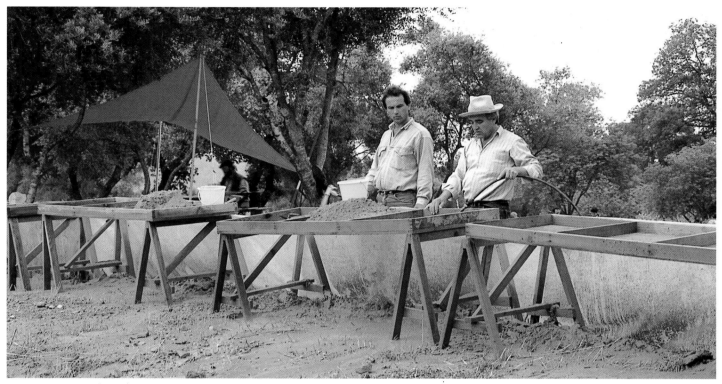

Archaeologists are interested in the small objects found at town sites as well as the buildings. Sieving through the "spoil" of an excavation is a good way of finding them.

AERIAL ARCHAEOLOGY

One of the best ways to locate a site is from the air. Many archaeologists take photographs of the landscape from airplanes and then study the pictures for any tell-tale signs of a site. These may be "shadow marks" caused by bumps and hollows on the surface that can be seen when the sun is low in the sky. The marks are often traces of buildings or pits beneath the surface. In plowed fields, aerial photographs can reveal "soil marks," which are brought to the surface as a result of the plowing.

Crops too can reveal evidence of sites beneath them: they will ripen faster and be lighter in color if there is a lack of moisture in the soil caused by hidden walls or foundations. On the other hand, pits or ditches under the ground will hold moisture and the crops above will be greener and grow taller than those surrounding them. These signs are called "crop marks" and are very easy to spot on aerial photographs.

Aerial photographs are also used to understand a site once it has been discovered. Old field boundaries, field strips, and ancient trackways invisible on the ground appear obvious when seen from the air.

OLYNTHUS AND PELLA

The settlement that tells us most about Greek housing is Olynthus in the Chalcidice region of northern Greece. In 348 B.C. King Philip of Macedonia accused Olynthus of sheltering his enemies and destroyed the city. The Greek orator Demosthenes said of the disaster: "Later generations will scarcely believe a city had been on this site." He was proven wrong—by archaeology.

Olynthus was partly excavated between 1928 and 1934 by an American team of archaeologists from the School of Classical Studies. They found that the inhabitants of Olynthus lived in small square houses with three or four rooms opening onto an internal courtyard. This helped keep out the noise and dirt from the busy streets. The north side of the courtyard—known as a *loggia*—was covered and designed to catch the low winter sun. The walls were made with sun-dried mud bricks, which are warm in the winter and cool in the summer. To prevent dampness, the walls were built on stone foundations and then plastered and painted.

A ground plan of a typical ancient Greek house. Excavations have revealed that such houses were built in blocks of ten, surrounded by streets on all sides.

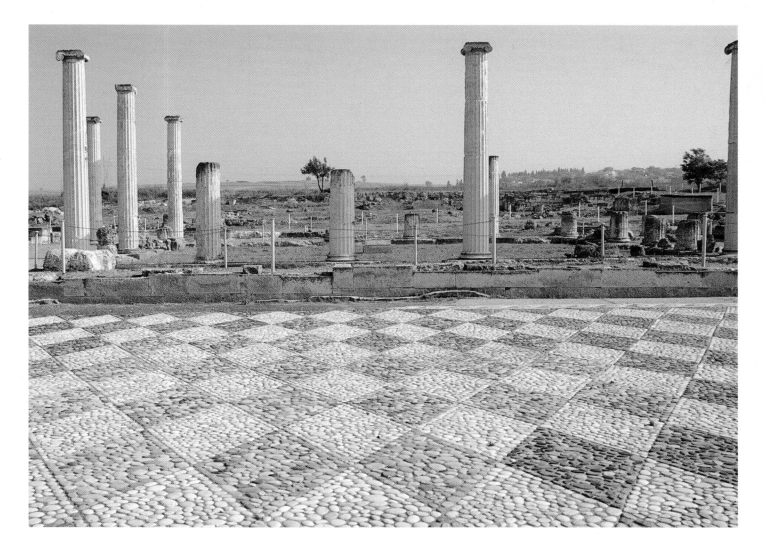

Many of the floors at Olynthus are decorated with pebble mosaics, and it seems that some houses were very expensive indeed. Archaeologists found a record of the sale of one: "Dionysion" bought it for 3,500 drachmas—the equivalent of 10 years of wages for a skilled workman of the time!

The mosaic floor of "The House of Dionysus" at Pella

The town of Pella is also in northern Greece and was also destroyed, this time by the Romans, in 168 B.C. It was said that so much treasure was plundered from Pella that the triumphal procession in Rome took a whole day. Excavation of Pella revealed an impressive town house known as the "House of the Lion Hunt"—the subject of a wonderful floor mosaic found there.

SANCTUARIES AND TEMPLES

Religion was a hugely important part of everyday life in ancient Greece, and the most sacred religious sites were the sanctuaries. Archaeological excavations have revealed that these were often highly complicated sites containing temples, treasuries, bronze and marble statues, theaters, gymnasia, and stadia (running tracks).

One of the most sacred sanctuaries was Delphi in central Greece. This was a sanctuary to the god Apollo and also the location of the famous "oracle," which was said to offer advice to people based on the wisdom of Apollo. High above the sanctuary is a stadium where the Pythian games were originally held every eight years. There is also a theater, which was used for musical contests. We know this because inscriptions of hymns to Apollo were discovered that were so well preserved that the hymns were revived in Greece in the 1930s!

The Tholos at Delphi. "Tholos" means "round building" or "dome," and this magnificent structure was constructed around 380 B.C. by the architect Theodorus entirely of marble and surrounded by 20 columns. Archaeologists are not sure what it was used for.

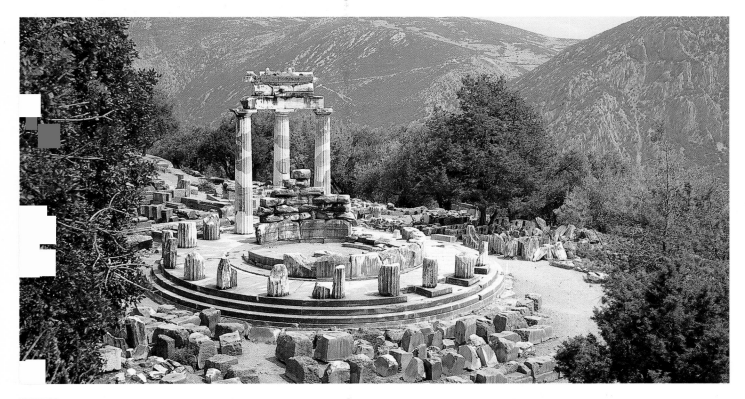

Excavations of Delphi, directed by the French School of Archaeology, began in 1892. The temple sanctuary was a large, roughly rectangular area enclosed by a wall. A sacred way lined with monuments wound up through the sanctuary to the temple of Apollo. The oracle was in a chamber at the rear of the temple.

Other sanctuaries have been found at Olympia (home of the Olympic Games), Epidaurus, Corinth, and many other places.

VOTIVE OFFERINGS

People who visited a sanctuary to ask the gods' blessing and favor had to offer a gift. Gifts were known as "votive offerings." People seeking cures for illness at the sanctuary of Corinth offered a terracotta (clay) model of the affected part of the body. Archaeologists have found models of legs, feet, arms, hands, eyes, and torsos.

One model, of a left hand, showed a large growth, perhaps a tumor or an abscess, providing evidence of one type of illness the god was asked to cure.

Making votive offerings was an important way to please the gods. Here a group of actors from Athens offer a play to Dionysus in their spring festival.

EXCAVATING THE SANCTUARIES

E ven using modern methods, the sanctuaries are not easy sites to excavate. Delphi, for example, is on different levels on the side of a steep hill, and each level has several layers, each of which has to be carefully examined before moving on to the next.

Despite careful cataloging and measurement of artifacts and buildings, some modern archaeologists feel that we still do not really understand how a sanctuary worked. This may be because useful clues in the form of archaeological evidence were lost or overlooked during previous excavations.

Excavations at the shrine of Pelops, Olympia. Pelops won a chariot race at Olympia by removing the pins from the wheels of his rival charioteers!

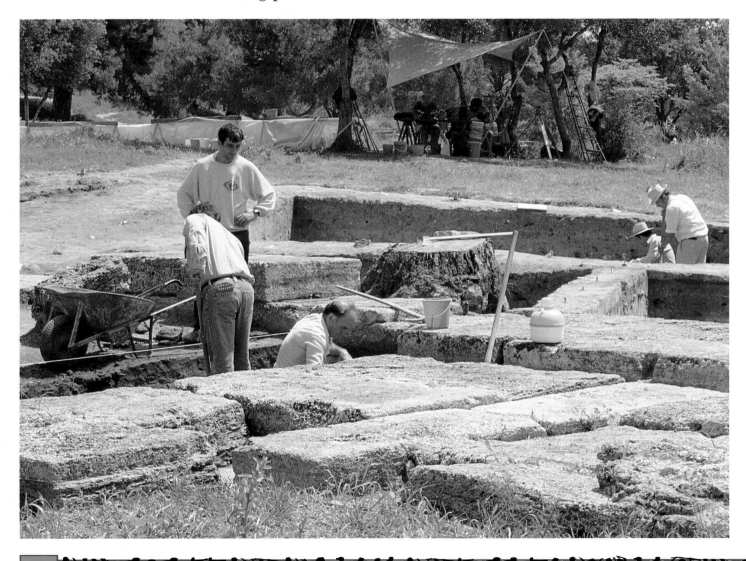

PROJECT: MAKE YOUR OWN DELPHIC TEMPLE

You will need:
12 cardboard tubes from paper towels
6 small toothpaste boxes
Cardboard from cereal packages
Package sealing tape
1 large flat side from a cardboard box,
  approx. 18 x 20 in. (45 x 50 cm) square
Paints
Paint brushes

1. Construct a four-sided box 7 x 20 x 9 in. (17 x 28 x 22 cm) and cut out a doorway at each of the narrow ends. Use the sealing tape to attach the box to the base. This is the "inner *cella*." Paint on a stonework effect.

2. Paint the 12 cardboard tubes with bright colors. Stick them around the *cella* to represent columns: four at each narrow end and two at each side.

3. Paint the toothpaste boxes and stick them along the tops of the columns. These form the base of the roof.

4. Cut out an appropriately sized piece of cardboard for the roof. Fold it down the middle and place it over the columns.

5. Check the angles at both ends of the temple and cut out two triangles for the pediments. Draw figures, color them, and attach them to the pediments. Paint the roof red.

1.

2–3.

4–5.

WARFARE

G reek military strength was based on two important things: the hoplite army made up of closed ranks of well-protected foot soldiers and naval strength from the lethal war galleys called triremes.

HOPLITES

O ur knowledge of hoplite armor comes from archaeology. Warrior graves have been discovered all over Greece, as well as marble carvings and paintings of soldiers on pottery. The most important piece of equipment was the shield, because it allowed the soldier to cover a large part of his own body and some of the body of the comrade on his left when in tight formation. Shields were about 30 in. (80 cm) in diameter and were faced and rimmed with bronze. The rest of the shield was probably made of wood or leather: only the bronze survives because wood and leather disintegrate and perish over time.

A hoplite's head was protected by a helmet beaten from a single sheet of bronze. Other equipment included leg-guards, chest and shoulder pieces, a sword, and a spear.

A superb suit of hoplite armor, from an eighth-century B.C. grave at Argos. The helmet and breastplate are both made of bronze. This is the oldest suit of armor to be found in Greece to date.

THE BATTLE OF MARATHON

One of the most famous battles of the Persian Wars (499–478 B.C.) was the battle of Marathon in 490 B.C. Although heavily outnumbered, the Greeks (made up of Athenian and Plataean warriors) managed to defeat the powerful Persian army. The Athenians lost 192 warriors in the fighting, and they were buried under a huge burial mound ("soros"), 33 ft. (10 m) high and 656 ft. (200 m) in circumference. The soros was excavated in 1890, and archaeologists discovered the ashes of cremated warriors, the bones of animal sacrifices, and some pottery.

In 1970, the smaller soros of the Plataean dead was discovered. Excavations revealed 11 skeletons of men in their twenties, one 12-year-old boy, and one man about 40, probably an officer. All this helped archaeologists understand the burial ceremonies of dead warriors and the types of offerings and sacrifices that were made to the gods at an ancient Greek warrior's funeral. Different types of swords, arrowheads, and bullet-shaped slingshots provided valuable clues about how the battle was fought.

Two hoplite warriors fighting. The bronze rail at the center of a hoplite's shield allowed him to hold it even if his hand was doing something else.

TRIREMES

Triremes were oar-powered warships famous for their speed. They helped the Greek city states beat the Persians at the battle of Salamis in 480 B.C. Evidence, such as inscriptions and the writings of Greek authors, shows that these ships had 170 oarsmen, which meant that they could reach speeds of up to 8 mph (13 km/h). This allowed them to attack enemy ships using a bronze-clad ram, which pierced their hulls and sank them.

THE *OLYMPIAS*: A TRIREME SAILS AGAIN

Historians and engineers recently used all the evidence they had collected about triremes to build one themselves and sail it around the Mediterranean. This helped them learn more about what triremes were like to sail and row, how fast they could go, how easily and quickly they could be turned around, and how far they could travel in a day.

The Olympias *at full speed. Besides being fighting platforms, the decks of a trireme offered protection for the rowers.*

The oarsmen were arranged on three levels along each side of the ship: 31 on the top level, 27 in the middle, and 27 at the bottom. The oars were prevented from colliding with one another by an outrigger for the top level of rowers so that their oars struck the water slightly farther out and at a steeper angle. Sails were used for power when the trireme was not in a battle.

PROJECT: MAKE YOUR OWN TRIREME

You will need:
A piece of cardboard 12 x 16 in.
  (50 x 40 cm)
Scissors
Paints
Scrap paper
Drinking straws

1. Draw one side of your trireme onto the cardboard. It needs to be about 14 in. (35 cm) long. Cut it out and then draw around the shape to make a second identical side. Use the scissors to punch the oarholes (in sets of three) into the hull. Glue the sides into a simple boat shape.

2. Put a piece of scrap paper over the top of the ship and draw the outline of the deck. Allow an extra $1/2$ in. (1 cm) all the way around the edge.

3. Cut out and paint the deck and the sides of the hull. Make small cuts around the edge of the deck shape, turn up the edge, and glue it into the hull.

4. Carefully split the ends of the straws and insert small pieces of cardboard for the paddles. Slide the oars into the oarholes.

5. Cut out a steering oar and stick it to the side of the ship at the stern (rear). Add a pointed ram made of cardboard and cut back the prow (front) to the correct shape. Add a curved piece of cardboard to the stern.

1.

2.

3.

4–5.

SCIENCE AND HEALTH

Classical Greece is justly famous for its scientific and medical ideas. Hippocrates (469–399 B.C.), who is often called the "father of medicine," pioneered the idea of scientifically observing a patient as a way of understanding disease. His ideas on diet and treatment are still regarded today as being thousands of years ahead of their time.

Archaeologists have found portable medical cases used by ancient Greek doctors when visiting their patients. They contained bronze instruments such as tongs, scalpels, spatulas, and spoons and had tiny compartments for different drugs. By serving in the army, many doctors became very experienced in treating wounds and broken bones. They were often called to the *palaistra* (the gymnasium or wrestling ground) to set broken arms or legs.

A Greek vase painting showing a doctor bleeding a man's arm. This was done to remove the "bad blood" or impurities from the patient.

THE SECRETS OF SKELETONS

Modern archaeological techniques help us study and learn about the health of ancient peoples and the environment in which they lived. Skeletons can reveal evidence about the age, sex, diet, and general health of people when they were alive.

The sex of a skeleton is usually identified by the size of the skull and the width of the pelvis. "Harris lines"—tiny cracks in the bones caused by famine, illness, or wounding—show when bone growth began and when it stopped. The position of the lines in relation to the long arm or leg bones tells archaeologists at what age in the person's life such problems occurred.

Skeletons of the ancient Greeks have revealed that many suffered from osteoarthritis—painful stiffness in the joints. This shows up in skeletons as wear and tear in the large weight-bearing joints of the knee, hip, and spine.

FACIAL RECONSTRUCTION

Archaeologists can use the skulls of people found at sites to reconstruct what their faces were like. A cast of the skull is made and then the depth of the muscle tissue calculated from the age and sex of the skeleton. Experts then use modeling clay to "bring the person to life." One of the most famous reconstructions is that of King Philip II of Macedonia, destroyer of Olynthus and father of Alexander the Great.

Richard Neave's remarkable reconstruction of the head of Philip II was made from the remains of a skull found in the royal tomb at Vergina, Macedonia. Philip's disfigured eye was probably the result of a sword blow during one of his many battles.

TRANSPORTATION

The development of transportation networks in ancient Greece came as a result of the geography. Despite the steep, craggy mountains, the ancient Greeks built roads, although the sheer size of the mountains made this a difficult and expensive task.

On flatter land, roads tended to be dirt tracks, and roadside accommodation was provided for travelers. We know this because a large hostel containing 160 rooms was excavated at the sanctuary of Epidaurus. Poor people usually walked from place to place. Richer people probably rode horses. A record of a horse being rented has survived and was discovered in Athens.

Because Greece is surrounded by water, merchant ships were used for carrying heavy cargoes over long and short distances. Ports were built on all the main islands and around the mainland to load or unload goods being delivered from all over the Mediterranean. Many harbor walls still in use today date back to the Classical Greek era—for example, those on the islands of Samos and Delos.

The remains of the hostel used by visitors to Epidaurus. Nearby was the important bath house where weary and dusty travelers cleaned up after their long journey.

A slow, heavy merchant ship with a faster, two-level warship. Note the sharp bronze ram, used to sink enemy ships.

Ancient Greek pottery paintings show that merchant ships came in all shapes and sizes but did have a number of similarities. Most were steered from the stern by one man holding two steering oars. They had rectangular sails attached to the central mast by a yard (beam of wood). By using the yard to turn the sail, it was possible to sail slightly into the wind, a technique known today as "tacking."

SHORTCUT BY SLIPWAY

An incredible example of ancient Greek technology and engineering was excavated on the isthmus (thin strip of land) between Attica and the Peloponnese that separates the Saronic Gulf from the Gulf of Corinth. Instead of sailing around the long way by sea, the ancient Greeks built a *diolkis*, or slipway, across the isthmus so that ships could be hauled across on carts pulled by oxen. Deep ruts caused by the cart wheels are still visible in the stone road.

THE KYRENIA SHIP

Underwater archaeology has helped archaeologists understand a lot more about ancient Greek merchant ships and their cargoes. One of the most exciting underwater discoveries was the "Kyrenia Ship," a fourth-century B.C. merchant ship found not far off Kyrenia, in Cyprus. Well-preserved in 100 ft. (30 m) of water, it was excavated in the late 1960s.

The cargo found on board was impressive: 404 amphorae (storage jars) of wine, 10,000 almonds, and 29 assorted millstones, which were probably used as ballast to keep the ship stable in the water. Four sets of clay jugs, cups, spoons, and plates indicated a crew of four men. The pottery was traced to the island of Rhodes, so this was probably the ship's home port. A coin found on board was dated to 306 B.C., so the last voyage of the Kyrenia Ship must have taken place after this date.

Divers carefully excavating a section of a wreck in the Mediterranean Sea. The sand and silt on the sea bed often preserve wood and leather objects.

Archaeologists have pieced together what they think were the ship's last moments. Eight spearheads, some embedded in the side of the hull, suggest that it was attacked, perhaps by pirates. It may be that the crew was taken prisoner to be sold as slaves, and the ship robbed of any valuable cargo before being sunk to destroy the evidence.

Today the Kyrenia Ship is preserved in polyethylene glycol (PEG) and is on display in the Kyrenia Crusader Castle.

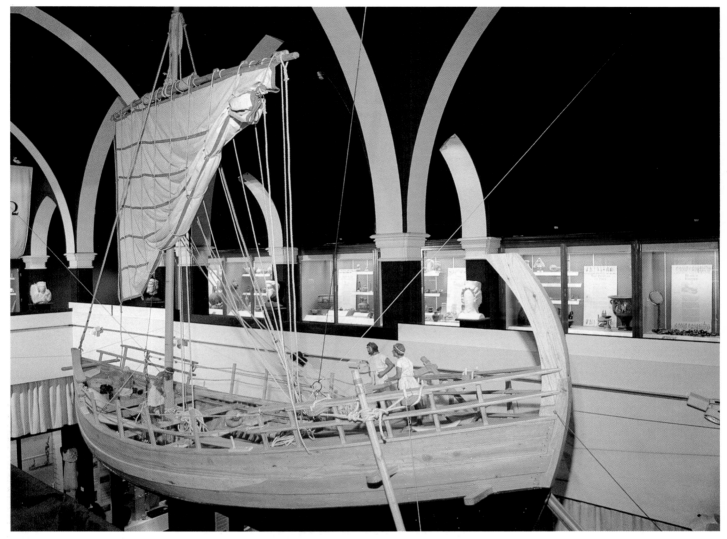

A model of the Kyrenia Ship, housed in the Manchester Museum, in England. Between 1982 and 1985, the Kyrenia II was built near Athens and was launched on August 22. In April 1986, this ship repeated Kyrenia's final voyage, averaging just over 2 knots.

CARBON DATING

All living things absorb carbon while they are alive, and after they die the amount of radioactivity in the carbon begins to decrease at a very uniform rate. Archaeologists can use a small sample of anything that once lived (wood, leather, bone, etc.) to measure the level of radioactivity in the carbon and find out how old the object is. Carbon dating is accurate to within 50–100 years either way, making it a very important archaeological tool. It was used to test timbers and foodstuffs from the Kyrenia Ship, giving an approximate date of 389 B.C.

THE MYSTERY OF LINEAR B

When Sir Arthur Evans was excavating Knossos in 1900, he discovered some clay tablets with strange inscriptions on them. He was to collect about 2,000 of these altogether, and he tried to decipher the writing, which he called "Linear B." He thought it "may well be some primitive sort of Greek," but got no further than that. Similar tablets were then found at the Mycenaean palace of Pylos in 1939 and at Mycenae in 1950.

Linear B remained a mystery until 1952 when a British architect named Michael Ventris finally cracked the code. He found that the script was an early form of Greek, and that the tablets were records of trade, listing goods, equipment, and people (presumably slaves).

A fragment of Linear B script from Mycenae. These tablets often list information about numbers of sheep, rams, goats, and pigs.

MICHAEL VENTRIS

The British born Michael Ventris (1922–1956) showed an early interest in Linear B when, as an 18-year-old, he daringly published an article about the Minoan language. In 1951 the Linear B tablets found at Pylos were published, and this gave Ventris plenty of examples to work on. In July 1952 he announced his theory that Linear B was an ancient form of Greek dating from about 1400 B.C.

Understanding Linear B was an important discovery because the tablets provided a huge amount of information about the ancient Greek world. For example, until the code was cracked by Ventris, archaeologists had no idea that flax (linen) was grown around Pylos or that it was important to the ancient Greeks. The tablets show that there was a large textile industry based on flax, which was traded around the Peloponnese. This area continued to produce flax right up to the twentieth century.

A black-figure vase dating from the sixth century B.C., showing cloth merchants at work, carefully weighing the bales of cloth

POTTERY

Archaeologists have found huge amounts of pottery at sites all over Greece. Sometimes many shards from the same pot are found together and the pot can be reconstructed.

Reconstructions have revealed that ancient Greek pottery was often very well made and beautifully painted. The two most popular types of pottery are known as "black figure" (a red pot decorated with black figures) and "red figure" (a black pot decorated with red figures). The detailed paintings on pottery have provided archaeologists with valuable information about religion, warfare, and everyday life in ancient Greece.

When pottery is excavated, it is necessary to wash it carefully before examination. Each piece is marked with the date and the position where it was found.

Pottery is useful to archaeologists in other ways too. By looking closely at the clay a pot was made from, they can discover where it was made. If a pot was found a long way from its place of manufacture—in southern Russia, for example—ancient Greek trade routes can be figured out.

By studying the way pots were made and their many different styles, a dating sequence can be established. This sequence becomes even more reliable when examples of pottery are found at a site that has a known date. For example, burned pottery found in Athens at the correct layer may have a connection with the Persian destruction of the city in 480 B.C. If so, the pottery can be correctly slotted into the dating sequence.

A dinos, or wine-mixing bowl, on a stand, made by Sophilos, one of the first well-known ancient Greek vase painters.

THERMOLUMINESCENCE

Pottery is made of clay, and the minerals found in clay store energy from any nuclear radiation it is exposed to. If clay is heated to above 932° F (500° C) (such as when a pot is fired to harden it) the stored energy is given off as light. This light is called thermoluminescence.

When the heating is finished the clay pot will begin to store energy again. Archaeologists use special scientific equipment to calculate when a pot was last heated, and hence when it was made.

PRESERVING THE PAST

Discovering sites and excavating artifacts from the ground is only part of an archaeologist's work. Sites and artifacts must be cared for and conserved for the future.

A serious problem facing the ancient monuments of Greece is the pressure of the modern world. The Acropolis is in grave danger from air pollution, which is damaging the surfaces of the marble monuments, and from tourism. The millions of tourists who visit every year are actually wearing away the rock with their feet. Traffic vibrations also cause damage to the monuments.

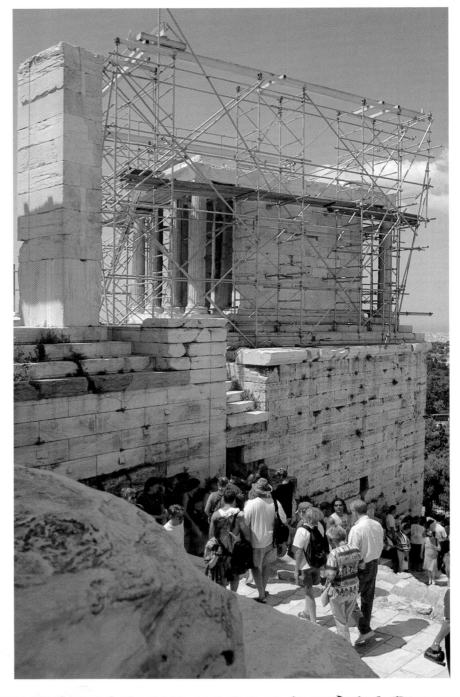

The temple of Athena Nike on the Acropolis undergoing important restoration work. Note the large number of tourists climbing up the rock.

Because of this, all of the remaining statues have been taken into the Acropolis Museum, and parts of the standing monuments have been protected by wooden roofs. Measures to try to reduce air pollution in Athens have been introduced. In an effort to try and reduce vibration, cars are no longer allowed to drive up to the base of the Acropolis. Sad to say, tourists are no longer allowed inside the monuments as they once were.

Long-term restoration work is currently taking place at the Erecthteion on the Acropolis. This impressive temple was built at the end of the fifth century B.C. to house a statue of Athena. The famous Porch of the Caryatids—statues of women holding up the roof—and the beautiful marble walls were in terrible condition by the late 1970s. Something had to be done to arrest and repair the damage. Lord Elgin had taken one of the Caryatids back to London, so part of the restoration process involved filling the empty space with a replica statue.

The beautiful marble Caryatid in splendid isolation in the British Museum, taken from her home in the Erecthteion by Lord Elgin.

WHAT NEXT?

Today, archaeologists working in Greece and her ancient colonies tend to combine different approaches. A site may require the painstaking work of field walking and surveying in one area, some small-scale excavation in another, and a major dig in yet another. Sometimes archaeologists deliberately leave a portion of a site unexcavated so that more advanced and as-yet uninvented techniques can be used to uncover its mysteries.

Archaeologists carefully scraping and brushing the surfaces of their trenches. Much of their work is slow and methodical, especially with fragile objects.

Modern technology is changing the way sites can be understood. A combination of field walking to turn up surface artifacts and the use of ground penetration radar over a site can produce computer maps of what lies beneath the ground with no need for excavation at all. This method has allowed archaeologists successfully to discover ancient roads, bridges, pottery kilns, wells, graves, wine presses, farmhouses, and even whole sanctuaries. However, sometimes excavation is still essential, as in "rescue archaeology," where a site is threatened by the building of a new road, an office building, or even a parking lot.

The Duveen Gallery in the British Museum, which houses the Elgin Marbles. Millions of visitors come here each year from all over the world.

For the people of Greece the issue of the Elgin Marbles, presently held at the British Museum in London, remains unresolved. Many people, both in Greece and the UK, feel that the Marbles should be returned home to Greece. The Greek government has been requesting them for years, but not until recently did popular opinion begin to agree. It may be that in the not too distant future the Elgin Marbles will be returned to the land where they were first made.

TIME LINES

ANCIENT GREEK TIME LINE (ALL DATES ARE B.C.)

ca.2600–1450	ca.1626	ca.1580–1400	ca.1450	ca.1375
Minoan civilization develops. Knossos built (see page 6–7)	Thera erupts with terrible results for Crete (see page 7)	On the Greek mainland, the Mycenaean civilization flourishes (see page 8)	Mycenaeans conquer Crete (see page 7)	Palace at Knossos destroyed

ca.776	From 650	499–478	ca.448–432	431–404
Olympic Games begin	Greek colonies started: the beginning of "Classical Greece" (see page 10)	Wars between the Greeks and the Persians	Parthenon built (see pages 16)	Peloponnesian War: Athens vs. Sparta

ARCHAEOLOGICAL TIME LINE (ALL DATES ARE A.D.)

1800–1805	1846	1866–1889	1870–1890	1882	1885
Lord Elgin in Athens (see page 17)	French School of Archaeology at Athens founded	National Archaeological Museum built in Athens	Schliemann excavates Troy (see pages 8–9)	American School of Classical Studies set up in Athens	British Archaeological School set up

ca.1250	ca.1125
Possible date for the Trojan Wars (see page 8)	Mycenae invaded by northern tribes. Beginning of the dark ages (see page 10)

338	336–323	30
Defeat of Greek city states by Philip II of Macedonia	Reign of Alexander the Great	Greece becomes part of Roman Empire

1896	1900	1928–1934	1931	1952	1977
First modern Olympic Games	Sir Arthur Evans begins excavating Knossos (see page 7)	American School excavates at Olynthus (see pages 20–21)	American School excavates the agora at Athens (see page 15)	Michael Ventris announces his theory about Linear B (see pages 36–37)	Discovery in Vergina of the tomb of Philip II of Macedonia (see page 31)

GLOSSARY

acropolis the highest and best defended part of an ancient Greek city.

agora the marketplace in ancient Greece.

artifacts objects, such as tools or pots, that help archaeologists find out how people lived.

Athena Greek goddess of war and arts and crafts. Athens was named after her.

cella the most sacred part of a temple or shrine.

city state (*polis*) a self-governing city and its surrounding area.

corrosion the wearing away of metal and other materials by chemical attack, for example, by air and water

crop marks marks that can be seen from the air in fields with crops, which show there may be remains beneath the soil.

"dark age" the period in ancient Greece after 1100 B.C. when much culture—such as writing—was lost.

democracy a political system that originated in Greece. Democracy means "rule by the people."

hoplite a Greek foot soldier armed with a spear and protected by a large shield.

Minoan of the civilization on Crete ca. 2600–1450 B.C. Sir Arthur Evans coined the term "Minoan" after the legendary King Minos.

Mycenae the city state of Mycenae, which was at its peak ca. 1400 B.C.

pediment low triangular wall between the pitched roof and columns at the narrow ends of large Greek buildings such as temples.

resistivity a way of "seeing into the ground" using electricity. Solid objects produce high resistance, while hollow areas produce low resistance.

shadow marks aerial photographs taken of the ground when the sun is low in the sky show up hollows and bumps that can betray the presence of buried features.

shard a piece of broken pottery or glass.

soil marks aerial photographs of plowed fields can reveal different soil colors, which may indicate the presence of a buried feature.

spoil the waste—soil and stones—from an excavation. It is usually dumped into a spoil heap, which is checked every evening for any artifacts that might have slipped through.

treasuries found in sanctuaries, these held the big votive offerings from the city states and individuals.

trireme a Greek warship, propelled by 170 oarsmen organized in three levels, hence the name.

votive offering an offering to the gods, in the hope of a blessing or a favor in return.

FURTHER INFORMATION

BOOKS

Dawson, Imogen. *Food and Feasts in Ancient Greece* (Food and Feasts). Parsippany, NJ: Silver Burdett Press, 1993.

Descamps-Lequime, Sophie & Venerey, Denise. *The Ancient Greeks: In the Land of the Gods* (Peoples of the Past.) Ridgefield, CT: The Millbrook Press, 1992.

Loverance, Rowena. *Ancient Greece* (See Through History). New York: Viking Children's Books, 1993.

Millard A. & S. Peach. *The Greeks* (Illustrated World History) Brookfield, CT: Millbrook Press, 1990.

Nardo, Don. *Ancient Greece* (World History.) San Diego: Lucent Books, 1994.

Pearson, Anne. *Everyday Life in Ancient Greece* (Clues to the Past). Danbury, CT: Franklin Watts, 1994.

Sauvain, Philip. *Over 2000 Years Ago in Ancient Greece* (History Detective.) Parsippany, NJ: Silver Burdett Press, 1992.

INDEX